D0535682

21st Century Skills **INNOVATION LIBRARY**

MAKERS
As Innovators

Solar Energy Projects

CHERRY LAKE PUBLISHING • ANN ARBOR, MICHIGAN

by Audrey Huggett

CHERRY
LAKE
Publishing

A Note to Adults: Please review the instructions for the activities in this book before allowing children to do them. Be sure to help them with any activities you do not think they can safely complete on their own.

A Note to Kids: Be sure to ask an adult for help with these activities when you need it. Always put your safety first!

Published in the United States of America by Cherry Lake Publishing
Ann Arbor, Michigan
www.cherrylakepublishing.com

Series Editor: Kristin Fontichiaro
Photo Credits: Cover and page 1, ©Jerry Meaden/tinyurl.com/z4pjj5r/CC BY 2.0; page 4, ©Ineta McParland/tinyurl.com/zp3j5gv/CC BY 2.0; page 5, ©Josh/tinyurl.com/zbq4k9t/CC BY-ND 2.0; ©Jennifer Boyer/tinyurl.com/hq6gvps/CC BY 2.0; page 8, ©Mike Mozart/tinyurl.com/glg7waf/CC BY 2.0; page 10, ©Aske Holst/tinyurl.com/hhzj9qb/CC BY 2.0; page 11, ©Michael Coghlan/tinyurl.com/q8p9dmr/CC BY-SA 2.0; page 12, ©Daderot/tinyurl.com/jqb2f57/CC0 1.0; page 13, ©Rocky Raybell/tinyurl.com/ j8mdye8/CC BY 2.0; page 15, ©Thangaraj Kumaravel/tinyurl.com/gvtfj6y/CC BY 2.0; page 16, ©Dvortygirl/tinyurl.com/zaojrqp/CC BY-SA 2.0; pages 19, 20, 22, 24, 27, and 28, Audrey Huggett

Library of Congress Cataloging-in-Publication Data
Names: Huggett, Audrey, author.
Title: Solar energy projects / by Audrey Huggett.
Other titles: 21st century skills innovation library. Makers as innovators.
Description: Ann Arbor, Michigan : Cherry Lake Publishing, [2016] | Series:
   Makers as innovators | Audience: Grades 4 to 6. | Includes bibliographical
   references and index.
Identifiers: LCCN 2015048101| ISBN 9781634714174 [lib. bdg.] |
   ISBN 9781634714334 [pbk.] | ISBN 9781634714259 [pdf] |
   ISBN 9781634714419 [ebook]
Subjects: LCSH: Solar energy—Juvenile literature.
Classification: LCC TJ810.3 .H84 2016 | DDC 621.47—dc23
LC record available at http://lccn.loc.gov/2015048101

Cherry Lake Publishing would like to acknowledge the work of the Partnership for 21st Century Learning. Please visit *www.p21.org* for more information.

Printed in the United States of America
Corporate Graphics
July 2016

Contents

Chapter 1

What Is Solar Energy?

The sun is an important part of our lives, even if we don't think about it every day. Its bright light allows us to see. It provides us with a huge amount of energy. In fact, the amount of sunlight that reaches Earth each hour is more than enough to satisfy the entire world's energy needs for a whole year.

Have you ever thought of sunlight as energy?

A tree takes energy from the sun and combines it with water from its roots to create oxygen, which is released into the air, and sugar, which fuels the tree's growth. This energy conversion is known as photosynthesis.

If you have ever gone outside on a sunny day, you've probably noticed the sun's rays warming your skin. Even on a cold day, the difference in temperature between standing in the sun and standing in the shade is often noticeable. That change in temperature is the energy in sunlight at work. Sunlight warms you when you stand directly in the path of the energy.

A plant can absorb energy from the sun through its leaves.

Art museums are extremely careful about where they hang their art. This is partly because they know how much energy the sun contains. Over time, exposure to direct sunlight can cause the colors of a painting to fade. As the various colors on a painting absorb and attract energy from the sun, they are affected by the energy and slowly lose some of their brightness.

Priceless works of art aren't the only thing affected by the sun's energy. You may have noticed that posters or pictures hanging on your wall might begin to look a little faded over time. You can do a simple experiment to see this effect firsthand. Use your computer to type a few words in large black type on a single sheet of paper. Print out two copies. Hang one on a wall in your home where it will be exposed to direct sunlight on a regular basis. Place the other one in a dark place. After a couple of months, the words on the paper hanging in the sun should begin to fade. Compare it to the one in the dark to see just how much it has changed. If you wait an entire year, you may see the words disappear almost completely!

Plants are the original pioneers of solar power. They use **photosynthesis** to convert sunlight and water into the food they need to live. If you cover up a plant so it can't get enough light, it will eventually die. Humans are not able to use photosynthesis. However, scientists have figured out how to turn sunlight into an energy source that can be used for a wide variety of purposes. We can convert sunlight into **thermal** energy to heat our homes. We can also convert it into electricity to power lights, computers, and other devices.

While people have experimented with making solar energy widely available since the early 1900s, interest in this power source has grown a lot in the past few years. This is mainly because it is better for the environment than most other energy sources. Unlike **fossil fuels**, which are created slowly over a long period of time, solar power is a renewable resource. This means it is a nearly unlimited source or energy.

Fossil fuels such as gasoline are a limited resource that will run out one day.

Why Do Energy Sources Matter?

Currently, 68 percent of the energy used in the United States comes from fossil fuels such as oil, coal, and natural gas. Fossil fuels get their name from the material they are made of—fossils. These substances are formed over millions of years from the bodies of living things. Even though fossil fuels occur naturally, we are using them up much more quickly than the planet can create them. Scientists agree that our supply of fossil fuels is limited. They will run out someday, though no one is quite sure when that will happen. We only have one planet, and finding renewable, clean energy sources is a great way to take care of it!

In addition to being readily accessible, solar power is a clean energy source. A clean energy source is one that creates few **by-products** when it is captured and stored. Burning fossil fuels for electricity leads to nasty outcomes like air pollution, water pollution, and even illness in humans. Fossil fuels can also require drilling into the planet's surface. Solar energy, on the other hand, can be collected simply by placing a panel in direct sunlight. Those concerned about the effects of **climate change** promote the use of energy sources that are both renewable and clean.

Even though solar energy is being used more often, there are still some challenges to the widespread use of the technology. One drawback is that we can't collect solar energy at night. The technology

As they burn fossil fuels to create electricity, power plants release gases that harm the planet.

may also not work well on cloudy days. To adjust for this, solar energy can be stored in special batteries and used when there is no light to collect.

Another problem is that the costs of installing devices used to capture solar energy can be high. To save money, many people look elsewhere for their energy needs. However, increased interest, technological advances, and support from many governments in recent years has caused the price of solar technology to begin dropping.

Chapter 2

How Solar Energy Works

We know energy from the sun is all around us, but how do we collect and use it? Solar energy is actually a very flexible energy. We can use devices to capture and store it. However, we can also use the energy directly from the sun without needing any machines.

Many people install solar panels on their homes to help reduce their use of fossil fuels.

Solar panels are probably the most well-known type of solar device. These devices are an example of something called active solar capture. Active solar capture occurs any time a mechanical device collects heat or light from the sun and converts it into usable energy. Solar panels perform **photovoltaic** power conversion. This is when light is converted into electricity.

To understand solar panels, you need to understand how light works. A single ray of light contains every color imaginable. We see different colors based on how much light is absorbed by an object. When light hits an object and all of the light is absorbed, we see black. When light hits an object and all of the light

Some innovators have even created solar-powered race cars.

A rainbow shows what light looks like when it is separated into its many colors.

is reflected, we see white. Have you ever noticed that some colors seem to attract more sunlight than others? If you think about this in terms of energy, it means that black objects absorb more energy than white ones. When we use solar panels, the goal is to

Tracking the Sun

Finding the best position for a solar panel is key for gathering solar energy. Each day, the sun travels in a consistent path across the sky from east to west. This means that different areas of your home get different amounts of light at different times of the day. Many people forget that the sun also moves from north to south in the sky. However, this change happens much more slowly. As our planet travels around the sun, different parts of it are closer to the sun at different times. This means that the noon sun in winter will be in a completely different position in the sky than the noon sun in summer. When deciding where to place a solar device, it's important to keep these factors in mind. Some parts of the world don't get enough sunlight for enough hours a day for solar power to be a reliable, consistent source of energy.

Think about which areas in your own home naturally get more light than others. A quick walk around the house can give you a basic idea of which areas are brightest and which are darkest. Knowing where these spots are will come in handy when you work on the projects ahead in this book.

collect the most energy possible. This is why they are colored black.

Another way of using solar energy is called passive solar capture. This method is used mainly when planning and constructing buildings. A passive solar building is designed to use the sun's natural warmth for heating. The most important part of a

The sun's position in the sky follows a different path in different parts of the world and at different times of the year.

passive solar building is its placement. Since the building is intended to naturally capture energy from the sun, it needs to be placed in a location that gets plenty of light.

Greenhouses stay warm by trapping solar energy inside.

Humans have long designed buildings to capture the passive energy of the sun. Greenhouses are one of the most familiar examples of this. These glass rooms or buildings are designed to capture heat without letting any warmth escape. They are usually built to help plants grow inside.

Keeping a building cool with passive solar capture
is as simple as blocking the sun's rays. Some high-tech
shades can raise and lower automatically depend-
ing on the sun's position. However, a simple curtain to
cover a window is also a form of passive cooling.

Chapter 3

Making Solar Energy at Home

A re you ready to try your hand at using solar energy? These experiments are a great place to get started.

Project 1: A Unique Angle

The sun's location in the sky changes over the course of the day and from season to season. By creating different angles of light with a flashlight, you can see the ways that the angle of the sun affects the energy in a single spot.

What you will need

- Large sheet of paper
- Tape
- Piece of string
- Flashlight
- Pencil

Shine your light at several different angles to
see how the beam changes shape.

Because we are using a flashlight in place of the
sun, you'll need to do this experiment in a dim room.
Start by taping the sheet of paper to the wall. Use
tape to attach one end of the string to the center of
the paper. Tie the other end of the string around your
flashlight. The string will ensure that we are compar-
ing the light from the flashlight at the same distance,
even as its angle changes.

Stand directly in front of the paper and turn on your flashlight. Shine it directly at the center of the paper, keeping the string pulled tight. Draw a circle around the area of brightest light on the paper. Now move the flashlight to a different angle, away from the center. Keep the string tight. Again, draw a circle around the area of brightest light. Repeat this at a few different angles.

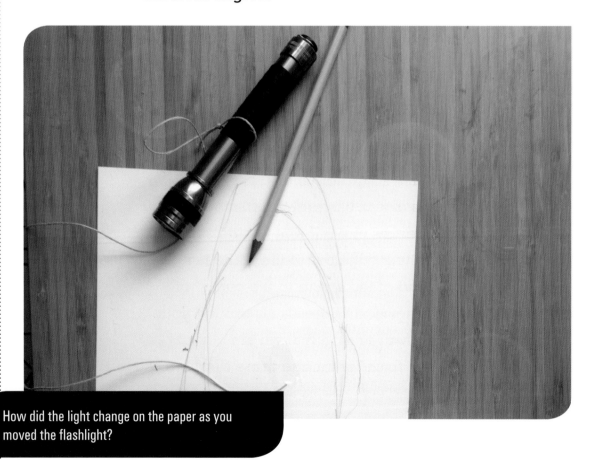

How did the light change on the paper as you moved the flashlight?

What do your circles tell you about the way light behaves? The distance from the paper and the intensity of the light remained the same throughout the experiment. However, the circles of light changed. In some cases, this change was probably huge.

Think about the way the beam of light changed as you moved the flashlight. It should have been at its brightest when the flashlight was positioned at a right angle from the paper, pointing straight at it. As you moved the flashlight, the beam spread out more. This made the light on the paper dimmer because the same amount of energy was being spread out over a larger area.

This diagram allows us to think about the amount of light that might hit a solar collector during the day. When the sun is directly overhead, the solar collector is being treated to a full dose of the sun's energy. However, as the sun moves across the sky, the solar collector receives less light and energy.

Project 2: Using Color to Attract Sunlight

Different colors absorb different amounts of light from the sun. This simple experiment is an easy way to figure out which colors attract the most energy.

What you will need

- Several colors of construction paper
- Several plastic cups of the same size and shape
- Several ice cubes
- Timer

We will test which colors attract the most sunlight by melting ice cubes. Your first step will be to make

Each color of paper should absorb light at a different rate.

the chambers for the ice cubes. You should use several different colors. Be sure to include black and white. You will need one cup for each color you want to test. Cover the opening of each cup with a sheet of construction paper. You should use only one color per cup.

Place the cups in a sunny location. Drop an ice cube in each cup, and then start your timer. Peek inside the cups every five minutes or so. Which ice cubes melt the fastest? How long did it take for your first ice cube to start melting?

Project 3: Create a Solar Oven

We've learned that solar energy is great at creating heat. One of the most obvious ways to use this heat is for cooking! This homemade solar oven can lightly toast small items, including marshmallows for s'mores.

What you will need
- Craft knife or box cutter (ask an adult to help)
- Empty cardboard box with lid
- Aluminum foil
- Glue stick
- Clear plastic wrap or two clear freezer bags cut along the seam

- Duct tape or masking tape
- Bamboo skewer, stick, or dowel
- Aluminum pie pan

Start by cutting a three-sided flap in the top of the box's lid. Be sure to leave a border of 1 to 2 inches (2.5 to 5 centimeters) around the flap. Cover the inside of the flap with foil, using the glue stick to hold it in

Your finished solar oven should look something like this.

place. Try to make the aluminum foil as smooth as possible. Next, cover the inside of the box with foil as well. Go over each side of the box with the glue stick before putting down the foil.

Gently lift up the flap of the box and tape a layer of the plastic wrap over the opening. Attach another layer of plastic wrap to the underside of the lid. These two layers of clear plastic will help keep the heat from the sun inside the oven, while allowing even more energy to enter the oven.

Poke a hole in the top of the lid for your stick to go into. Then carefully tape the skewer, stick, or dowel to the edge of the flap. The stick will act as a prop to keep the flap open.

Now it's time to cook! Place your oven in a sunny spot with the flap propped open to direct sunlight into the box. Give the oven about 30 minutes to preheat. Once it is good and hot, you can place your food on an aluminum pie pan and put it inside the oven. One easy thing to make in the oven is a s'more!

S'more Recipe
- Graham crackers
- Thin chocolate bar
- Marshmallows

S'mores are easy to make. First, break two graham crackers in half. Place one marshmallow on each graham cracker square, then place them on the aluminum pie pan. Put the pan inside the preheated solar oven. The next part requires some patience. Let the marshmallows and graham crackers sit for 30 to 60 minutes. The time really depends on what type of day it is and how much sunlight is hitting the oven. Your goal is for the marshmallows to be squishy when poked.

Once your marshmallows are done cooking, open up the oven and place a piece of chocolate on each marshmallow. Close up the oven and let everything sit for about 5 to 10 minutes longer. The chocolate will start to melt. While you wait, break two more graham crackers in half. These graham cracker squares will become the tops of the s'mores. Once the chocolate is ready, remove the pie pan from the oven. Place a graham cracker square on top of each stack. Push down gently until the marshmallow squishes down. Now they're ready to eat!

Project 4: Using the Sun to Collect Water
In this experiment, we'll learn how to **distill** water using the power of the sun. If you ever end up

Try to place the glass as close as possible to the center of the bowl.

stranded on a desert island without fresh water, this is a great trick to keep up your sleeve! This simple distillation technique can be used in any situation where you might need to create clean water from salt water.

What you will need

- Bowl
- Water
- Salt
- Cup
- Clear plastic wrap
- Small stone, marble, or coin

When gathering materials for this experiment, make sure your cup is short enough to sit about 2 inches (5 cm) lower than the edge of the bowl.

Start by filling the bowl about halfway with water. Stir in a couple of tablespoons of salt. Place the cup in the middle of the bowl. The cup should rise out of the salt water a little bit. Next, completely cover the bowl with plastic wrap. Place your stone, marble, or coin in the middle of the plastic wrap, directly above the cup.

Keep an eye on the water in your bowl as the sunlight heats it up.

This should cause the plastic wrap to dip down in the middle—make sure it does not slip off the edges of the bowl. To start distilling water, position your bowl in a sunny area and let it sit for a little while. The longer you leave it alone, the more water you will collect.

The sun heats the water in the bowl. The water that would normally **evaporate** into the air is trapped inside the bowl by the clear plastic wrap. You will see it collect on the underside of the plastic as it distills. The salt is too heavy to evaporate. It remains behind in the bowl of water. Meanwhile, the weight on top of the plastic wrap encourages the water to move to the center of the bowl. Clean water naturally drops into the cup. After you've let a little bit of water collect in the cup, go ahead and taste it! It's safe to drink, and it should taste fresh, not salty!

If you completed all the activities in this book, you probably learned a lot about the way solar energy works. However, there is still a lot more to discover. Read more about solar energy and try some experiments of your own. One day, you could make the next big innovation in solar power!

Glossary

by-products (BYE-prah-dukts) things left over after making or doing something

climate change (KLYE-mit CHAYNJ) global warming and other changes in weather patterns that are happening because of human activity

distill (di-STIL) to purify a liquid by heating it, collecting the steam, and then letting it cool until it takes a liquid form again

evaporate (i-VAP-uh-rate) to turn into a vapor or gas

fossil fuels (FAH-suhl FYOO-uhlz) coal, oil, or natural gas, formed from the remains of prehistoric plants and animals

photosynthesis (foh-toh-SIN-thi-sis) a chemical process by which green plants and some other living things make their food from solar energy

photovoltaic (fo-toh-vol-TAY-ik) relating to the process of turning solar energy into electricity

thermal (THUR-muhl) of or having to do with heat or holding in heat

Find Out More

BOOKS

Bow, James. *Energy from the Sun: Solar Power*. New York: Crabtree Publishing, 2016.

Taylor-Butler, Christine. *Super Cool Science Experiments: Solar Energy*. Ann Arbor, MI: Cherry Lake Publishing, 2010.

Vogel, Julia. *Solar Power*. Ann Arbor, MI: Cherry Lake Publishing, 2013.

WEB SITES

NASA—Climate Kids

http://climatekids.nasa.gov
Learn about the environment and the way our energy use affects it through hands-on activities, games, and educational videos.

U.S. Energy Information Administration— Energy Kids

www.eia.gov/kids
Check out this interactive site with plenty of information and activities focused on teaching kids about the way energy is used.

Index

About the Author

Audrey Huggett graduated from the University of Michigan, where she studied how the maker movement can be brought to libraries.